HANDLING
STRESS

BIBLE STUDY

HOPE FOR THE HEART BIBLE STUDIES

June Hunt

ROSE PUBLISHING/ASPIRE PRESS

Peabody, Massachusetts

ROSE PUBLISHING/ASPIRE PRESS

Hope For The Heart Bible Studies
Handling Stress Bible Study

Published by Aspire Press, an imprint of
Hendrickson Publishers Marketing, LLC
P. O. Box 3473
Peabody, Massachusetts 01961-3473 USA
www.HendricksonRose.com

Get inspiration via email, sign up at
www.aspirepress.com

Unless otherwise indicated, all Scriptures taken from the Holy Bible, New International Version®, NIV®. Copyright © 1973, 1978, 1984, 2011 by Biblica, Inc.™ Used by permission of Zondervan. All rights reserved worldwide. www.zondervan.com The "NIV" and "New International Version" are trademarks registered in the United States Patent and Trademark Office by Biblica, Inc.™

Scripture quotations marked ESV are from The Holy Bible, English Standard Version® (ESV®), copyright © 2001 by Crossway, a publishing ministry of Good News Publishers. Used by permission. All rights reserved.

The views and opinions expressed in this book are those of the author(s) and do not necessarily express the views of Aspire Press, nor is this book intended to be a substitute for mental health treatment or professional counseling.

The information in this resource is intended as guidelines for healthy living. Please consult qualified medical, legal, pastoral, and psychological professionals regarding individual concerns.

For more information on Hope For The Heart, visit www.hopefortheheart.org or call 1-800-488-HOPE (4673).

Printed in the United States of America
010517VP

CONTENTS

ABOUT THIS BIBLE STUDY 4

A NOTE TO GROUP LEADERS 7

FOUR POINTS OF GOD'S PLAN 12

Session 1 13
Definitions of Stress

Session 2 29
Characteristics of Stress

Session 3 47
Causes of Stress, PART 1

Session 4 61
Causes of Stress, PART 2

Session 5 73
Biblical Steps to Solution, PART 1

Session 6 91
Biblical Steps to Solution, PART 2

About This Bible Study

THANK YOU. Sincerely. Thanks for taking the time and making the effort to invest in the study of God's Word with God's people. The apostle John wrote that he had "no greater joy than to hear that my children are walking in the truth" (3 John 4). At HOPE FOR THE HEART, our joy comes from seeing God use our materials to help His children walk in the truth.

OUR FOUNDATION

God's Word is our sure and steady anchor. We believe the Bible is *inspired* by God (He authored it through human writers), *inerrant* (completely true), *infallible* (totally trustworthy), and the *final authority* on all matters of life and faith. This study will give you *biblical* insight on the topic of stress.

WHAT TO EXPECT IN THIS BIBLE STUDY

The overall flow of this topical Bible study looks at stress from four angles: Definitions, Characteristics, Causes, and Biblical Steps to Solution.

- The **DEFINITIONS** section orients you to the topic by laying the foundation for a broad understanding of stress from a biblical and emotional standpoint. It answers the question: What does it mean?

- The **CHARACTERISTICS** section spotlights various aspects that are often associated with stress, giving a deeper understanding to the topic. It answers the question: What does it look like?

- The **CAUSES** section identifies the physical, emotional, and spiritual sources of stress. It answers the question: What causes it?

- The **BIBLICAL STEPS TO SOLUTION** sections provide action plans designed to help you—and help you help others—deal with stress from a scriptural point of view. It answers the question: What can you do about it?

The individual sessions contain narrative, biblical teaching, and discussion questions for group interaction and personal application. We sought to strike a balance between engaging content, biblical truth, and practical application.

GUIDELINES

Applying the following biblical principles will help you get the most out of this Bible-based study as you seek to live a life pleasing to the Lord.

- **PRAY** – "Unless the LORD builds the house, the builders labor in vain" (Psalm 127:1). Any progress in spiritual growth comes from the Lord's helping hand, so soak your study in prayer. We need to depend on God's wisdom to study, think, and apply His Word to our lives.

- **PREPARE** – Even ants prepare and gather food in the harvest (Proverbs 6:6–8). As with most activities in life, you will get out of it as much as you put into it. You will reap what you sow (Galatians 6:7). Realize, the more you prepare, the more fruit you produce.

- **PARTICIPATE** – Change takes place in the context of community. Come to each session ready to ask questions, engage with others, and seek God's help. And "do everything in love" (1 Corinthians 16:14).

- **PRACTICE** – James says, "Do not merely listen to the word, and so deceive yourselves. Do what it says" (James 1:22). Ultimately, this Bible study is designed to impact your life.

- **PASS IT ON!** – The Bible describes a spiritual leader who "set his heart to study the Law of the LORD, and to do it and to teach his statutes and rules" (Ezra 7:10 ESV). Notice the progression: *study . . . do . . . teach*. That progression is what we want for your journey. We pray that God will use the biblical truths contained in this material to change your life and then to help you help others! In this way, the Lord's work will lead to more and more changed lives.

OUR PRAYER

At HOPE FOR THE HEART, we pray that the biblical truths within these pages will give you the hope and help you need to handle the challenges in your life. And we pray that God will reveal Himself and His will to you through this study of Scripture to make you more like Jesus. Finally, we pray that God's Spirit will strengthen you, guide you, comfort you, and equip you to live a life that honors Jesus Christ.

A Note to Group Leaders

"Do your best to present yourself to God as one approved, a worker who does not need to be ashamed and who correctly handles the word of truth."

2 TIMOTHY 2:15

THANK YOU for leading this group. Your care and commitment to the members doesn't go unnoticed by God. Through this study, God will use you to do His work: to comfort, to encourage, to challenge, and even to bring people to saving faith in Christ. For your reference, we've included a gospel message on page 12 to assist you in bringing people to Christ. The following are some helpful tips for leading the sessions.

TIPS FOR LEADERS

- **PRAY** – Ask God to guide you, the members, and your time together as a group. Invite the group members to share prayer requests each week.

- **PREPARE** – Look over the sessions before you lead. Familiarize yourself with the content and find specific points of emphasis for your group.

- **CARE** – Show the members you are interested in their lives, their opinions, and their struggles. People will be more willing to share if you show them you care.

- **LISTEN** – Listen to the Lord's leading and the members' responses. Ask follow-up questions. A listening ear is often more meaningful than a good piece of advice.

- **GUIDE** – You don't have to "teach" the material. Your role is to *facilitate group discussion*: ask questions, clarify confusion, and engage the group members.

BEFORE THE FIRST MEETING

Schedule

- Determine the size of the group. Keep in mind that people tend to share more freely and develop genuine intimacy in smaller groups.

- Pick a time and place that works well for everyone.

- Decide how long each session will run. Sessions shouldn't take more than an hour or hour and a half.

- Gather the group members' contact information. Decide the best method of communicating (phone, text, e-mail, etc.) with them outside of the group meeting.

Set Expectations

- CONFIDENTIALITY – Communicate that what is shared in the group needs to stay in the group.

- RESPECTFULNESS – Emphasize the importance of respecting each other's opinions, experiences, boundaries, and time.

- PRAYER – Decide how you want to handle prayer requests. If you take prayer requests during group time, factor in how much time that will take during the session. It may be more effective to gather requests on note cards during the sessions or have members e-mail them during the week.

AT THE FIRST MEETING

Welcome

- Thank the members of your group for coming.

- Introduce yourself and allow others to introduce themselves.

- Explain the overall structure of study (Definitions, Characteristics, Causes, and Biblical Steps to Solution), including the discussion/application questions.

- Pray for God's wisdom and guidance as you begin this study.

LEADING EACH SESSION

Overview

- Summarize and answer any lingering questions from the previous session.

- Give a broad overview of what will be covered in each session.

How to Encourage Participation

- PRAY. Ask God to help the members share openly and honestly about their struggles. Some people may find it overwhelming to share openly with people they may not know very well. Pray for God's direction and that He would help build trust within the group.

- EXPRESS GRATITUDE AND APPRECIATION. Thank the members for coming and for their willingness to talk.

- **SPEAK FIRST.** The leader's willingness to share often sets the pace and depth of the group. Therefore, it is important that you, as the leader, begin the first few sessions by sharing from your own experience. This eases the pressure of the other members to be the first to talk. The group members will feel more comfortable sharing as the sessions progress. By the third or fourth session, you can ask others to share first.

- **ASK QUESTIONS.** Most of the questions in the study are open-ended. Avoid yes/no questions. Ask follow-up and clarifying questions so you can understand exactly what the members mean.

- **RESPECT TIME.** Be mindful of the clock and respectful of the members' time. Do your best to start and end on time.

- **RESPECT BOUNDARIES.** Some members share more easily than others. Don't force anyone to share who doesn't want to. Trust takes time to build.

Dealing with Difficulties

- You may not have an answer to every question or issue that arises. That's okay. Simply admit that you don't know and commit to finding an answer.

- Be assertive. Some people are more talkative than others, so it is important to limit the amount of time each person shares so everyone has a chance to speak. You can do this by saying something like: "I know this is a very important topic and I want to make sure everyone has a chance to speak, so I'm going to ask that everyone would please be brief when sharing." If someone tries to dominate the conversation, thank them for sharing, then invite others to speak. You can offer a non-condemning statement such as: "Good, thank you for sharing. Who else would like to share?" Or, "I'd like to make sure everyone has a chance to speak. Who would like to go next?"

- Sometimes people may not know how to answer a question or aren't ready to share their answer. Give the group time to think and process the material. Be okay with silence. Rephrasing the question can also be helpful.

- If someone misses a session, contact that person during the week. Let them know you noticed they weren't there and that you missed them.

WRAPPING UP

- Thank the group for their participation.

- Provide a brief summary of what the next session will cover.

- Encourage them to study the material for the next session during the week.

- Close in prayer. Thank God for the work He is doing in the group and in each person's life.

We are grateful to God for your commitment to lead this group. May God bless you as you guide His people toward the truth—truth that sets us free!

*"If [your gift] is to lead,
do it diligently."*

Romans 12:8

FOUR POINTS OF GOD'S PLAN

The gospel is central to all we do at Hope For The Heart. More than anything, we want you to know the saving love and grace of Jesus Christ. The following shows God's plan of salvation for you!

#1 GOD'S PURPOSE FOR YOU IS SALVATION.

God sent Jesus Christ to earth to express His love for you, save you, forgive your sins, empower you to have victory over sin, and to enable you to live a fulfilled life (John 3:16–17; 10:10).

#2 YOUR PROBLEM IS SIN.

Sin is living independently of God's standard—knowing what is right, but choosing what is wrong (James 4:17). The penalty of sin is spiritual death, eternal separation from God (Isaiah 59:2; Romans 6:23).

#3 GOD'S PROVISION FOR YOU IS THE SAVIOR.

Jesus died on the cross to personally pay the penalty for your sins (Romans 5:8).

#4 YOUR PART IS SURRENDER.

Place your faith in (rely on) Jesus Christ as your personal Lord and Savior and reject your "good works" as a means of earning God's approval (Ephesians 2:8–9). You can tell God that you want to surrender your life to Christ in a simple, heartfelt prayer like this: "God, I want a real relationship with You. Please forgive me for my sins. Jesus, thank You for dying on the cross to pay the penalty for my sins. Come into my life and be my Lord and Savior. In Your holy name I pray. Amen."

WHAT CAN YOU EXPECT NOW?

When you surrender your life to Christ, God empowers you to live a life pleasing to Him (2 Peter 1:3–4). Jesus assures those who believe with these words: "Very truly I tell you, whoever hears my word and believes him who sent me has eternal life and will not be judged but has crossed over from death to life" (John 5:24).

DEFINITIONS OF STRESS

"Come to me, all you who are weary and burdened, and I will give you rest. Take my yoke upon you and learn from me, for I am gentle and humble in heart, and you will find rest for your souls. For my yoke is easy and my burden is light."

MATTHEW 11:28–30

Are you *stressed out* and barreling down the road to *burnout*? Stress can be a motivator or a mean taskmaster, unceasingly pressuring you and relentlessly threatening your peace and joy. You can feel like you're carrying the weight of the world on your shoulders. But it is a great relief when you realize the truth that your burden is carried by Someone else.

Jesus invites you: "Come to me, all you who are weary and burdened, and I will give you rest" (Matthew 11:28). God's will for your life is not continual stress, but rather confident rest. You can be confident that in every circumstance He is at work within you. God wants your stress to send you straight into the Savior's arms.

Stress can be a motivator or a mean taskmaster.

Abraham Lincoln: President, Emancipator, Stressed Out

The sixteenth president of the United States, Abraham Lincoln, is a man universally acknowledged to be no stranger to stress. It repeatedly pulled Lincoln down to the depths of despair.

Lincoln grew up with stress as a constant companion, emotionally troubling him and eventually enveloping him. An impoverished and tragic childhood—marked by the deaths of his mother, aunt, uncle, and beloved sister, as well as the neglect of an emotionally absent father—proved to be the stressful opening chapter to a life that would be punctuated by pain and anguish. As an adult, *melancholy* became a common word to describe Lincoln's demeanor. He lived in a state of sadness that drew both attention and sympathy of those around him.

In this session, we'll look at definitions of stress, unhealthy stress, and stress from a biblical point of view.

The apostle Paul was also no stranger to stress. In his letter to the Corinthians, he describes numerous external circumstances and internal struggles that caused a great deal of pressure in his life. Yet despite all of his stress, he knew what to do with it. He knew he could turn to the Lord and receive His help and grace for any situation.

Read about the apostle Paul's stress in 2 Corinthians 11:23–31. What stressors was he facing when he wrote these words?

....

....

....

....

....

....

Also, look at 2 Corinthians 12:7–10 to see how Paul handled his stress. What did he do with it, and how did God respond to him?

....

....

....

....

....

....

What Is Stress?

STRESS IS . . .

External pressure causing physical, mental, or emotional strain.

- Example: "The stress from that heavy truck caused the old wooden bridge to collapse."

   "People cry out under a load of oppression; they plead for relief from the arm of the powerful" (Job 35:9).

Self-induced internal pressure causing physical, mental, emotional, or spiritual strain.

- Example: "The stress of striving for perfectionism leaves me mentally and emotionally exhausted."

   "By one sacrifice he [God] has made perfect forever those who are being made holy" (Hebrews 10:14).

Internal resistance responding to outside pressure.

- Example: "The stress in my lower back was caused by lifting heavy boxes."

   "My back is filled with searing pain; there is no health in my body" (Psalm 38:7).

Negative pressure resulting in distress, danger, or destruction.

- Example: "The stress from many harsh winters destroyed the fruit trees in my back yard."

  ". . . when calamity overtakes you like a storm, when disaster sweeps over you like a whirlwind, when distress and trouble overwhelm you" (Proverbs 1:27).

Positive pressure producing motivation and movement.

- Example: "The stress of needing to support my family caused me to seek a better job."

  "The appetite of laborers works for them; their hunger drives them on" (Proverbs 16:26).

Write from the Heart

What stresses you out? Sometimes we find reasons to avoid talking with another person or group about our struggles. We may want to avoid burdening someone else or we may have a hard time developing trust. But it is important to find a safe place to share our struggles.

A positive first step could be opening up to God about your stress. Read Matthew 11:28–30 and take a few minutes to write a prayer to God about the stress that is threatening your peace and joy.

Name some *positive* and *negative* pressures (i.e., stressors) in your life.

Positive pressures:

....

....

....

....

....

....

....

Negative pressures:

....

....

....

....

....

....

....

What Is Unhealthy Stress?

Anna Mayes Rutledge, a blue-eyed, blonde-haired, lovely young woman, was the apple of Abraham Lincoln's eye. She was the picture of health, until an epidemic swept across rural Illinois. Anna became debilitated with what doctors then described as "bilious fever."

Lincoln tended to the sick, built coffins, and assisted with burials. When Anna became sick, the health crisis became personal and distressing. Lincoln regularly visited Anna's bedside. Stress came at Lincoln from seemingly all sides for months. Prior to the epidemic, his nerves were frazzled from his obsessive, day-and-night study of law.

Lincoln put his own health at risk through personal neglect. This led to an emaciated appearance. One resident commented, "His best friends were afraid that he would craze himself—make himself derange[d]."[1] And sadly, their fears ultimately came true.

In August of 1835, the untimely death of Anna Rutledge dealt the final blow to Lincoln's fragile emotional and mental states. He was already battered and bruised by unhealthy stress. After her death, he became unstable.

On the cold and wet the day of Anna's funeral, Lincoln was distressed about rain falling on her grave. The cold, gloomy weather was detrimental to his emotional health throughout his life. It often served as the culminating factor that pushed him over the edge. He once wrote that bad weather had proved "to be very severe on defective nerves."[2]

Following Anna's death, Lincoln was seen wandering in nearby woods, gun in hand, admittedly contemplating suicide. His friends had to literally lock him up inside their home to prevent him from killing himself. People began to murmur one word about Lincoln: *crazy.*

UNHEALTHY STRESS . . .

- *Refers* more to the duration of stress over a considerable period of time.

- *Includes* external or internal pressure that God does not intend for us to experience.

- *Causes* detrimental effects to the body, soul, and spirit.

- *Stretches* us beyond the threshold of our physical, mental, and emotional limits that God established within us to protect from overload.

- *Plunges* us past a saturation point where nothing can be added without something else being eliminated.

Write from the Heart

Read how the Bible describes David's stress in Psalm 22:1. How did he feel?

....

....

....

....

....

....

Now, review the explanation of what unhealthy stress does to us. Does this describe you or anyone you know? List some specific ways you've seen unhealthy stress have a negative impact on you or someone you know.

....

....

....

....

....

....

What Does Scripture Say about Stress?

As a young boy, Lincoln was grounded in Scripture. His mother, Nancy, sat him on her lap and read from the family Bible. The Ten Commandments were a focal passage, evidenced by Nancy's final words to her nine-year-old son: "Abe, I'm going to leave you now and I shall not return. I want you to be kind to your father and live as I have taught you. Love your heavenly Father and keep His commandments."[3]

Lincoln's mother died in her mid-thirties from an infectious disease known as "milk sick." His stepmother, Sarah Bush, built upon Nancy's foundation. She faithfully took young Abe to Pigeon Creek Hard Shell Baptist Church every Sunday. Lincoln heard the Word of God. Lincoln read the Word of God. However, there is no evidence until later in life that he turned to the Word of God to find solace from his stress.

DISTRESS IN THE BIBLE

- *Distress* "implies an external and usually temporary cause of great physical or mental strain and stress."[4]

  "There will be trouble and distress for every human being who does evil" (Romans 2:9).

- *Distress* can be the result of severe, self-induced, internal stress.

  "See, LORD, how distressed I am! I am in torment within, and in my heart I am disturbed, for I have been most rebellious" (Lamentations 1:20).

- ***Distress*** is a state of anguish, vexation, or affliction.

  "While Paul was waiting for them in Athens, he was greatly distressed to see that the city was full of idols" (Acts 17:16).

- ***Distress*** is a word used over 100 times in the Bible (NIV) to describe negative stress.

  It most often pictures the negative result that pressure and pain can have on the heart.

  The apostle Paul wrote to those whom he deeply loved in the young Corinthian church—those who had severely rebelled against him, but had later sincerely repented.

  "For I wrote you out of great distress and anguish of heart and with many tears, not to grieve you but to let you know the depth of my love for you" (2 Corinthians 2:4).

- ***Distress*** is often a translation from the Hebrew word *tsarah*, which means "straits, distress."[5]

  The word means distress, anguish, or affliction in a spiritual or psychological sense.

  Due to the jealous rage of Joseph's ten older brothers, his life was in severe jeopardy. And despite his distressful pleas, the brothers sold him as a slave and he was carted off to Egypt. Years later, the brothers found themselves in the depth of distress. Because of the severe famine in Israel, the brothers traveled to Egypt in an attempt to buy grain. But when they came upon a stressful predicament, they reflected on what they had done to Joseph many years before and wondered if their cruel treatment of Joseph was the cause of their distress.

  "We saw how distressed he [Joseph] was when he pleaded with us for his life, but we would not listen; that is why this distress has come on us" (Genesis 42:21).

Write from the Heart

Read Psalm 22:19–22. How do you typically cope with stress? What Bible passages and promises are particularly comforting and meaningful to you when you are stressed?

Discussion/Application Questions

1. Describe how a Bible character or personal role model handled stress in either positive or negative ways.

   ....

   ....

   ....

2. Is stress more of a motivator or mean taskmaster to you? Explain why.

   ....

   ....

   ....

3. Remember, Jesus invites you to "Come to me, all you who are weary and burdened, and I will give you rest" (Matthew 11:28). What stresses do you need to bring before the Lord, your Burden Bearer? Write about them in a prayer to God.

   ....

   ....

   ....

   ....

   ....

Notes

"Now may the Lord of peace himself give you
peace at all times and in every way."
2 Thessalonians 3:16

CHARACTERISTICS OF STRESS

"We are hard pressed on every side, but not crushed; perplexed, but not in despair; persecuted, but not abandoned; struck down, but not destroyed."

2 CORINTHIANS 4:8–9

Stages of Stress

Abraham Lincoln referred to it as "that fatal first of Jany. 41."[6]

It was January 1, 1841. A great deal of mystery exists even today about what precisely drove Lincoln to a complete breakdown. It's clear there were multiple stressors in his life both personally and professionally. Historians can only speculate as to what pushed him over the edge.

It may have been that the once bustling Illinois economy had come to a disastrous standstill by the end of 1840. The internal improvements package to which Lincoln had so closely aligned himself was a failure. State debt exceeded $13.6 million, and bank-issued currency had lost all value. Lincoln's reputation was tanking along with the economy. That was a bitter pill to swallow for a man who so highly valued character and a strong public presence.[7]

In this session, we'll look at the stages of stress and symptoms of burnout.

THE FOUR STAGES OF STRESS

Today, we all have varying amounts of stress. Contrary to what many think, a moderate amount of stress can be helpful. For a student, the moderate stress of an exam typically provides the motivation to study. Likewise, with no homework to turn in and no regular tests to take, many students would be unmotivated to study. But if there is too much stress, the possibility of burnout is ever present.

The following describes the four stages of stress.

STAGE 1: No Light. Insufficient Stress.
No motivation to move responsibly.

STAGE 2: Green Light. Positive Stress.
Motivation to move responsibly.

STAGE 3: Yellow Light. Negative Stress.
Motivational warning signs to slow down movement.

STAGE 4: Red Light. Burnout.
Movement stops and repair is necessary.

A moderate amount of stress can be helpful. Too much stress can cause burnout.

"I call on the LORD in my distress, and he answers me."

PSALM 120:1

Write from the Heart

Does stress tend to motivate you or immobilize you? In what ways?

....

....

....

....

....

....

....

Read Psalm 120:1 and write down the first step you should take when facing a stressful situation.

....

....

....

....

....

....

....

What Characterizes the Stages of Stress?

"Lincoln," one observer noted, "went crazy as a loon."[8]

Razors were removed from his room. Knives and other sharp objects were taken from him. Lincoln was reeling. Fears of a further tarnished reputation consumed him. But it was affairs of the heart—not affairs of the state—that sent his emotions into overdrive.

Lincoln was engaged to Mary Todd, but his heart belonged to another, a graceful, curly-haired blonde named Matilda Edwards. Mary recognized Lincoln's affections for Matilda. She eventually released him from the engagement, but not without exacting a significant amount of guilt upon the lovelorn Lincoln.

And many believe the breakup with Mary Todd was the catalyst for "that fatal first of Jany. 41." Lincoln's conscience was deeply stressed over the fact that his heart would wander while under a matrimonial agreement.

Lincoln could relate to the psalmist:

> *"My guilt has overwhelmed me like a burden too heavy to bear."*
>
> PSALM 38:4

STAGE 1: NO LIGHT

With insufficient stress to encourage an individual to act responsibly, you will find that the person . . .

- Avoids responsibility
- Has poor relationships
- Is not productive
- Has no energy
- Experiences depression
- Has no purpose
- Lacks perspective on life
- Has a short temper

STAGE 2: GREEN LIGHT

Positive stress pushes you to proper maintenance. When there is sufficient positive stress, you will find that a person . . .

- Faces responsibility
- Has responsible relationships
- Is productive
- Has energy
- Experiences peace
- Has fulfillment of purpose
- Has a positive perspective
- Has patience

STAGE 3: YELLOW LIGHT

The warning signs of stress are like the amber lights on a traffic signal—they caution you to be on the alert, to slow down, and to be prepared for upcoming change. The following are physical warning signs of stress.

- Tension headaches, stomach aches
- Muscle aches, back aches
- Heavy sighing, rapid breathing
- High blood pressure
- Hyperalertness, anxiousness
- Restlessness, weight gain or loss
- Loss of sleep, excessive sleep
- Lack of concentration, constant worrying
- Indecisiveness, poor judgment
- Irritability, agitation

Positive stress pushes you to proper maintenance.

STAGE 4: RED LIGHT

Burnout is not God's will for you. It may just be that you have not processed the stresses of life in a godly way. Instead of living at Stage 2, a person becomes . . .

- Overwhelmed by responsibility
- Withdrawn from relationships
- Minimally productive
- Easily fatigued, nervous
- Depressed (lack of enthusiasm), moody
- Purposeless, disinterested in sex
- Without perspective, but with erratic eating and sleeping patterns
- Impatient, easily angered

Burnout is not God's will for you.

Write from the Heart

Which stage of stress do you most identify with in this season of your life? Explain.

....

....

....

....

....

....

....

....

....

....

....

....

....

....

....

....

Burnout

Lincoln was committed to honor and integrity. His turbulent emotions concerning the breakup with Mary Todd can be traced in part to the gravity of a matrimonial contract in nineteenth-century America. Legally binding, the rejected party had the right to seek damages. Lincoln himself had successfully served as the attorney in a "breach of promise" suit. The weightiness of a marriage pledge in the mid-1800s may also have contributed to "that fatal first of Jany. 41."

Following the breakup, Lincoln was in a cathartic state of self-analysis. He lost confidence in his ability to maintain resolve since he hadn't followed through and married Mary Todd. He wrote to his longtime friend Joshua Speed: "I must regain my confidence in my own ability to keep my resolves when they are made. In that ability you know, I once prided myself as the only, or at least the chief, gem of my character; that gem I lost—how, and when, you too well know. I have not yet regained it; and until I do, I cannot trust myself in any matter of much importance."[9]

Lincoln ended up marrying Mary Todd on November 4, 1842. One observer noted he "looked and acted as if he was going to the Slaughter."[10]

CHECKLIST FOR BURNOUT

The following checklist can help you identify the level of stress in your life. Put a check mark (√) next to the statements that currently apply to you.

Checklist for Burnout

Emotional Symptoms

- ○ I am plagued with guilt over not being as responsible or committed as I should be.
- ○ I feel apathetic and anxious.
- ○ I feel depressed.
- ○ I feel I don't do things as well as I could and should.
- ○ I have a great deal of self-doubt.
- ○ I have a sense of helplessness.
- ○ I have a sense of hopelessness.
- ○ I have decreased self-esteem.
- ○ I have difficulty concentrating.
- ○ I have feelings of confusion.
- ○ I have feelings of disenchantment.
- ○ I have feelings of disorientation.
- ○ I have feelings of disillusionment or failure.
- ○ I have increased irritability.
- ○ I have less time and energy for relationships.
- ○ I have uncharacteristic anger, cynicism, and negativism.

Physical Symptoms

- ○ I am susceptible to almost every cold and virus.
- ○ I eat and snack excessively.
- ○ I feel tired and lifeless most of the time.
- ○ I generally feel nervous and unsettled.
- ○ I grind my teeth at night.

Checklist for Burnout

○ I have a rapid pulse.

○ I have allergies or asthma.

○ I have difficulty relaxing.

○ I have frequent, severe headaches.

○ I have high blood pressure.

○ I have indigestion often.

○ I have lost or gained a lot of weight.

○ I have lower back pain.

○ I have shortness of breath.

○ I have tightness in my neck and shoulders.

○ I have trouble sleeping at night.

○ I often have cold hands and sweating palms.

○ I often have diarrhea or constipation.

Spiritual Symptoms

○ I am apathetic toward Scripture.

○ I am feeling more and more desperate to improve my situation.

○ I am losing confidence in God to help me.

○ I fail to recognize my own limits much of the time.

○ I feel I am in a spiritual vacuum.

○ I feel I am on my own.

○ I feel I have lost perspective on life.

○ I feel God has given up on me.

○ I feel like giving up on myself.

○ I rarely pray or have quiet time anymore.

It is normal to experience some of these symptoms. Look over where you put check marks. How many did you check? Are your symptoms of stress primarily emotional, physical, or spiritual? Or are they a blend of the types of symptoms? If you are concerned with how many statements you checked, you may need to evaluate how you are responding to the pressures in your life. You may also need to see a health-care professional, counselor, and/or pastor to discuss the effects of stress in your life.

The Bible says . . .

> *"A heart at peace gives*
> *life to the body."*
>
> PROVERBS 14:30

Write from the Heart

In Psalm 31:9–13, King David describes his stress in great detail. As you read this passage, make a list of symptoms of stress and burnout that David experienced.

. . . .

. . . .

. . . .

. . . .

. . . .

. . . .

In Psalm 31:14, 23–24 David describes his response to his stress. What did he do, and what does he tell us to do with our stress? Lastly, what does God do for those experiencing stress? See verses 19–22.

. . . .

. . . .

. . . .

. . . .

. . . .

. . . .

Discussion/Application Questions

1. Looking back on the Stages of Stress, describe how stress is used positively (i.e., to motivate people to action). What are some ways that stress can motivate people?

2. How has stress affected your relationships?

3. On a scale of 1 to 10 (1 being very low and 10 being extremely high), how stressful is your life right now? Who can you talk to about your stress?

....

....

....

....

....

....

....

4. Is anyone in your life burned out or on the verge of burnout? Write down some practical ways you can reach out to that person this week.

....

....

....

....

....

....

....

Notes

"Now may the Lord of peace himself give you
peace at all times and in every way."
2 Thessalonians 3:16

SESSION 3

CAUSES OF STRESS
PART 1

"When hard pressed, I cried to the LORD;
he brought me into a spacious place."

PSALM 118:5

No Shortage of Stress

While there is widespread speculation that Abraham Lincoln's initial breakup with Mary Todd prompted the "fatal first," there was no shortage of other stressful events in Lincoln's life that could have contributed to his emotional breakdown.

On January 1, 1841, Joshua Speed ended his business ties in Springfield, Illinois. Lincoln faced the prospect that his loyal, longtime companion might move away. And Speed may have been accompanied by someone precious to Lincoln. On the final evening of the leap year of 1840, there was a tradition for men to propose marriage.

Matilda Edwards captured the heart of another besides Lincoln—Joshua Speed. Did Lincoln learn of a proposal that "fatal first"?[11] In the midst of so much stress, there was One to whom Lincoln later turned, but not in January 1841.

In this session, we'll look at seven causes of stress and common responses to stress.

The Seven Classic Causes of Stress

1. CONFLICT [12]

Reasons you can experience conflict:

- Opposing values of family and friends
- Unresolved anger in relationships
- Unrealistic expectations of others
- Lack of open communication in relationships

Paul was met with extreme opposition from others.

"Are they servants of Christ? (I am out of my mind to talk like this.) I am more. I have worked much harder, been in prison more frequently, been flogged more severely, and been exposed to death again and again. Five times I received from the Jews the forty lashes minus one" (2 Corinthians 11:23–24).

2. CRISIS

Reasons you can experience crisis:

- Death of a friend or family member
- Separation or divorce
- Severe illness or sudden handicap
- Sudden or severe financial difficulties

Paul was shipwrecked and often in extreme danger.

"Three times I was beaten with rods, once I was pelted with stones, three times I was shipwrecked, I spent a night and a day in the open sea, I have been constantly on the move. I have been in danger from rivers, in danger from bandits, in danger from my fellow Jews, in danger from Gentiles; in danger in the city, in danger in the country, in danger at sea; and in danger from false believers" (2 Corinthians 11:25–26).

3. CHANGE

Reasons you can go through change:

- Change in environment or employment
- Change in financial or marital status
- Change in cultural or spiritual values
- Change in sleeping and health habits

Paul was constantly on the move, often going without sleep.

"I have been constantly on the move. . . . I have labored and toiled and have often gone without sleep; I have known hunger and thirst and have often gone without food; I have been cold and naked" (2 Corinthians 11:26–27).

4. CONDEMNATION

Reasons you can experience condemnation:

- Rejection by significant others

- Lack of support from coworkers

- Betrayal of a friend

- False accusations by family members

Paul was rejected and betrayed by the Gentiles and by his own people.

"I have been in danger from rivers, in danger from bandits, in danger from my fellow Jews, in danger from Gentiles; in danger in the city, in danger in the country, in danger at sea; and in danger from false believers" (2 Corinthians 11:26).

5. CONCERNS

Reasons you can carry concern:

- Unsaved or rebellious loved ones

- Unpredictable or uncertain future

- Recent or frequent fear of failures

- Perfectionism or excessive attention to details

Paul carried the daily pressure of concern for the churches.

"Besides everything else, I face daily the pressure of my concern for all the churches" (2 Corinthians 11:28).

6. COMPETITION

Reasons you can experience competition:

- Self-acceptance based on superior performance

- Comparisons between family, friends, or coworkers

- Envy or jealousy among neighbors or business associates

- Significance or security based on outperforming others

Paul chose to boast only in his weaknesses.

"If I must boast, I will boast of the things that show my weakness" (2 Corinthians 11:30).

7. CONSCIENCE

Reasons you can challenge conscience:

- Self, others, or things seem more important than God.

- Self-effort is perceived as the best way of meeting needs.

- Personal needs eclipse the needs of others.

- Acknowledgment of sin is considered an admission of weakness.

Paul was secure in his integrity before the Lord.

"The God and Father of the Lord Jesus, who is to be praised forever, knows that I am not lying" (2 Corinthians 11:31).

Write from the Heart

Of the seven classic causes of stress, which do you think create stress most often in your life? Choose one or two and explain why.

....

....

....

....

....

....

....

Read Jesus' words in Matthew 6:25–34. What encouragement do you find from what He says about stress and worry?

....

....

....

....

....

....

....

What Increases Stress?

YOUR MENTAL RESPONSE

Mental stress is caused by the way you think about or interpret events.[13]

- If you dwell on losing your job, you will feel stress.

- If you dwell on God's faithfulness to provide, He will replace your stress with His peace.

Do you have a positive or a negative outlook? If you dwell on negative thoughts, you can turn almost anything, even good circumstances, into stress. This is why God wants you to meditate on what is pure and good.

"Whatever is true, whatever is noble, whatever is right, whatever is pure, whatever is lovely, whatever is admirable—if anything is excellent or praiseworthy— think about such things."

PHILIPPIANS 4:8

If you dwell on negative thoughts, you can turn almost anything into stress.

YOUR EMOTIONAL RESPONSE

Emotional stress is caused by the way you process your thoughts.[14]

- If you think bitter thoughts, you will feel bitter emotions.

- If you think forgiving thoughts, you will feel forgiveness in your heart.

Although feelings need to be recognized and acknowledged, they are basically a product of your thinking, and they can be controlled. Emotional immaturity makes you a prisoner to your feelings and keeps you chained to undue stress.

Jesus said . . .

"Peace I leave with you; my peace I give you. I do not give to you as the world gives. Do not let your hearts be troubled and do not be afraid."

JOHN 14:27

YOUR PHYSICAL RESPONSE

Physical stress is caused by the way your body automatically responds to external pressure.[15]

- If you mentally dwell on your difficulties, you can develop physical fatigue.

- If you trust God for His timing, He provides you peace— mental, emotional, and physical peace.

If pressure is not dealt with in a healthy way, you become susceptible to a variety of physical problems. Prolonged stress can result in harmful physical reactions, such as elevated blood pressure and increased cholesterol levels. The Bible reveals that many of the consequences of stress can be avoided if you keep His Word in your heart.

"Do not let them [God's words of wisdom] out of your sight, keep them within your heart; for they are life to those who find them and health to one's whole body."
PROVERBS 4:21–22

YOUR SPIRITUAL RESPONSE

Spiritual stress is caused by the way you view God, His involvement in your life, and His sovereignty over your life.

- If you believe God is indifferent to you and powerless to work in your life and circumstances, you will have a crisis of faith.

- If you believe Him to be a loving Father, Helper, Friend, and Healer with infinite power to work on your behalf, you will enter into His rest and receive His peace.

In his famous book, *Knowledge of the Holy*, pastor and author A. W. Tozer wrote, "What comes into our minds when we think about God is the most important thing about us." Consider that the Bible describes God as the "God of hope" who gives us His peace (Romans 15:13).

Write from the Heart

How do you view God when you are stressed?

. . . .

. . . .

. . . .

. . . .

. . . .

. . . .

. . . .

Read Romans 15:13. Based on this verse, what will God do to help you overcome the stressors in your life? What's your part?

. . . .

. . . .

. . . .

. . . .

. . . .

. . . .

. . . .

Discussion/Application Questions

1. How we handle stress is often a learned behavior—from family, friends, or culture. Describe some ways that culture influences how people understand and respond to stress. What does culture say people should do with their stress?

    ....

    ....

    ....

    ....

    ....

    ....

2. How did your family and friends deal with stress? How has their behavior influenced how you handle stress? What has your church (past or present) taught you about stress?

    ....

    ....

    ....

    ....

    ....

    ....

3. Identify something in your life at present that is causing you stress. Describe your mental, emotional, and physical response to that stress.

....

....

....

....

....

....

4. God wants to help you overcome stress in your own life and also use you to help others deal with their stress. Write out a prayer telling God about your stress or that of a loved one. What is one thing you can do this week to relieve stress in your life and in their life?

....

....

....

....

....

....

....

Notes

"Now may the Lord of peace himself give you
peace at all times and in every way."
2 Thessalonians 3:16

CAUSES OF STRESS
PART 2

*"Cast your cares on the LORD and he
will sustain you; he will never let
the righteous be shaken."*

PSALM 55:22

The Dreaded Winter

Uncertain circumstances increased stress in Lincoln's life, but there was one constant that could be counted on to drag him down to the emotional dregs—the dreaded winter. It was one season of the year that continually blew a chill over his tormented soul. The winter of 1840–1841 was unusually bitter cold.

A friend of Lincoln's said it was colder in Illinois than anyone could remember. A newcomer to the state made the following observation: "I am sure I have seen colder weather in Connecticut. But I have never seen a place where cold is to be dreaded so much."[16] Lincoln was accustomed to that "dread," and it impacted his emotions every year.

In this session, we'll look at common stressors and the root cause of stress.

What Are Typical Stressors?

Situations and pressures that cause stress are referred to as stressors.

LIFE TRANSITIONS

Each stage of life has its own stressors.

- Learning to crawl, walk, talk

- Being potty trained, making friends, sharing with others

- Having unmet needs, wants, desires

- Dealing with siblings, attending school, dating

- Going to college, finding a job, getting married

- Moving, buying a house, having children

- Receiving a promotion, changing jobs, losing a job

- Experiencing an empty nest, infidelity, divorce, widowhood

- Taking care of elderly parents, illness, disability

- Retiring, poor health, grieving the death of significant others

DAILY HASSLES

While life-changing events cause major stress, it is often the daily hassles that impact people the most.

- Dealing with deadlines, demands, difficult people

- Encountering traffic, road rage, workplace politics

- Exhausting work, social schedule, church commitments

- Meeting needs of family, friends, employers

- Making phone calls, drafting letters, writing e-mails, texting, keeping up with social media

- Planning schedules, preparing meals, staying in shape

- Running errands, paying bills, resolving family problems

- Maintaining cars, house repairs, yard work

- Buying clothes, stocking up on supplies, helping children with homework

- Misplacing keys, losing wallet, losing sleep

INTERNAL FACTORS

Our emotions and our internal reaction to our external circumstances can also create stress.

- Fearing uncertainties in life

- Engaging in negative self-talk

- Nurturing a pessimistic outlook

- Exhibiting a critical spirit

- Lacking faith in a loving, all-powerful God

- Entertaining unrealistic expectations

- Refusing to forgive

- Resenting responsibilities

- Possessing phobias or addictions

- Harboring anger

COMPATIBILITY CONFLICTS

Stress is an individual, subjective experience. What one person finds stressful, another person finds invigorating.

- Avoiding vs. enjoying crowds

- Fearing vs. craving attention

- Collapsing vs. thriving under pressure

- Eluding vs. embracing confrontation

- Ignoring vs. providing caregiving

- Monopolizing vs. minimizing conversations

- Dodging vs. pursuing physical activity

- Causing vs. solving problems

- Deferring vs. making decisions

- Pleasing others vs. pleasing self

In reality, there are innumerable possible stressors in life because any event that is considered threatening, difficult to manage, or produces excessive pressure can result in stress. Individual beliefs, attitudes, interpretations, perceptions, and experiences influence what becomes stressful to a particular person. Therefore, it is critical that the first signs of stress or distress be met with a reality check. Identifying the truth behind our reactions to events in life is the starting place for turning destructive distress into constructive action. The psalmist clearly shows how important truth is to God:

"Behold, you delight in truth in the inward being, and you teach me wisdom in the secret heart."

PSALM 51:6 ESV

Write from the Heart

Describe some of the daily hassles that stress you out. Name at least one internal stressor and one external stressor.

....

....

....

....

....

....

In Psalm 55, the writer describes some of the internal and external stressors he is dealing with. Take a moment and observe what the psalmist experiences and write down what you learn from Psalm 55 about how to handle stress. What encouragement do you receive from verse 22?

....

....

....

....

....

....

What Is the Root Cause of Stress?

Joshua Speed, the ever-concerned friend, witnessed Lincoln repeatedly respond negatively to severe stress. Speed challenged him after his second breakdown to respond differently: You must rally or die. It became a pivotal chapter in Lincoln's life, an awakening that stirred Lincoln to aspire to greatness.

Lincoln told Speed that he was not afraid to die, but he had an "irrepressible desire" to make a great contribution to the people of his generation, to "so impress himself upon them as to link his name with something that would redound to the interest of his fellow man."[17]

Lincoln was beginning to move from a wrong belief about stress to a right belief about stress, and one day he would turn to God to help him carry the crushing burden of an entire nation.

Wrong Belief	Right Belief
"My life is out of control. I feel helpless to cope with all this stress in my life."	"God has allowed this stress in my life to bless me and to reveal my weaknesses. I am grateful for the pressures that have pressed me closer to Him and caused me to allow Christ to be my strength."

*"'My [Jesus'] grace is sufficient for you, for
my power is made perfect in weakness.'*

*Therefore I [Paul] will boast all the more gladly
about my weaknesses, so that Christ's
power may rest on me.*

*That is why, for Christ's sake, I delight in
weaknesses, in insults, in hardships,
in persecutions, in difficulties.*

For when I am weak, then I am strong."

2 CORINTHIANS 12:9–10

Write from the Heart

Describe a time when a stressful situation brought you closer to the Lord. Was there a prayer, a practice, or a passage of Scripture that was particularly helpful in relieving the stress you felt during that time?

....

....

....

....

....

....

For someone who is experiencing stress, what help and hope does 2 Corinthians 12:9–10 offer?

....

....

....

....

....

....

....

Discussion/Application Questions

1. How has technology (computers, smart phones, social media, etc.) influenced how people handle stress? In what ways has it helped people deal with stress and in what ways has it created stress?

....

....

....

....

....

....

2. We're often stressed out because we worry. We give in to negative self-talk and believe lies rather than the truths found in Scripture. What negative self-talk do you tend to give in to when you're feeling stressed? (Example: "I'm inadequate. I don't have what it takes to solve this problem.")

....

....

....

....

....

....

3. Having exposed some of the lies and negative messages, try to identify the source of them. Where did you learn them? What relationships, experiences, or environments have influenced you to believe some of the lies or negative messages?

....

....

....

....

....

....

....

4. What truths, promises, or specific passages from Scripture speak to the particular lies and negative messages that often influence you?

....

....

....

....

....

....

....

Notes

"Now may the Lord of peace himself give you
peace at all times and in every way."
2 Thessalonians 3:16

BIBLICAL STEPS TO SOLUTION
PART 1

"For everything that was written in the past was written to teach us, so that through the endurance taught in the Scriptures and the encouragement they provide we might have hope."

ROMANS 15:4

A Kindred Spirit

One topic dominated the political conversation in the 1860 presidential race: slavery. It was the line in the sand that clearly divided the north from the south. By the time Lincoln was elected president of the *United* States of America, *division* was already in the air.

Southerners considered the election of an antislavery candidate a signal—it's time to secede. Not a moment's time was wasted. About 10,000 volunteer soldiers were recruited and equipped in South Carolina. Georgia put $1 million on the table to fund a war and Louisiana approved $500,000 for guns and confederate fighters.[18] Before long, eight more states joined the initial trio that seceded and a full-scale civil war now painfully preoccupied the incoming president.

During his most desperate time, Lincoln sought rest, guidance, and empowerment from God. Following a devastating Union army defeat at Fredericksburg, Virginia, Lincoln stressfully paced the floor of his office and moaned repeatedly in grief and anguish, "What has God put me in this place for?"[19]

The dressmaker of Lincoln's wife recounted an insightful turn of events concerning the dejected president's source of strength and solace. Lincoln, appearing even more stressed and burdened than usual, collapsed on a sofa and reached for a Bible. Within 15 minutes the dressmaker witnessed an incredible change in his countenance. Hope and new resolve were written all over his face. Curious as to what precisely Lincoln was reading, she subtly peered over his shoulder and discovered—the book of Job.[20] The story of Job is the story of man who was well-acquainted with stress and suffering. Lincoln seemingly had found a kindred spirit with Job.

Write from the Heart

Read 2 Corinthians 1:3–4. What do you learn from these verses about helping others when they are stressed out and hurting? Who in your life needs your help to work through the suffering or stress they're experiencing? What can you do to help them?

In this session, we'll look at how to conquer stress and how to stop stress with biblical truth.

How to Conquer Stress

After you experience excessive wear and tear, and you know what conditions contribute to your stress, what action can you take? How can you conquer the classic causes of stress? How can the pressures in your life be used to press you closer to the Lord?

> *"This is a trustworthy saying that deserves full acceptance. That is why we labor and strive, because we have put our hope in the living God, who is the Savior of all people, and especially of those who believe."*
>
> 1 Timothy 4:9–10

1. CONFLICT

How you can conquer conflict:

- Accept one another's differences and focus on common goals.
- Resolve past anger and let go of present grudges.
- Avoid unrealistic expectations of others.
- Speak openly and honestly in relationships.

Paul encouraged the church at Rome:

"May the God who gives endurance and encouragement give you the same attitude of mind toward each other that Christ Jesus had, so that with one mind and one voice you may glorify the God and Father of our Lord Jesus Christ. Accept one another, then, just as Christ accepted you, in order to bring praise to God" (Romans 15:5–7).

2. CRISIS

How you can conquer crisis:

- Accept God's sovereign rule over life and death.

- Trust God's leadership in all relationship difficulties.

- Depend on God's sufficiency in physical trials.

- Rely on God's comfort and peace when blindsided by trauma.

King David acknowledged the sovereignty of God in his own life:

"All the days ordained for me were written in your book before one of them came to be" (Psalm 139:16).

3. CHANGE

How you can conquer change:

- View change as natural, constant, and ordained by God.

- Accept unwelcome changes as occasions to deepen trust in God.

- Welcome change as an opportunity to learn and grow.

- Consider physical changes as challenges to conquer and opportunities to develop Christlike character.

Daniel praised God as a change agent:

"Praise be to the name of God for ever and ever; wisdom and power are his. He changes times and seasons; he deposes kings and raises up others. He gives wisdom to the wise and knowledge to the discerning" (Daniel 2:20–21).

4. CONDEMNATION

How you can conquer condemnation:

- Realize there is no condemnation for those who are in Christ.

- Cultivate a spirit of cooperation and teamwork.

- Maintain faithfulness in the face of unfaithfulness.

- Extend forgiveness and speak the truth.

Paul encouraged the early Christian church to walk in forgiveness:

"Bear with each other and forgive one another if any of you has a grievance against someone. Forgive as the Lord forgave you" (Colossians 3:13).

5. CONCERNS

How you can conquer concerns:

- Entrust loved ones to the Lord's care and protection.

- Trust God with tomorrow and enjoy life today.

- Learn from failures; they can be more valuable than successes.

- Put away perfectionism and focus on improvement while aiming for excellence.

Jesus addressed the concerns of life:

"So do not worry, saying, 'What shall we eat?' or 'What shall we drink?' or 'What shall we wear?' . . . But seek first his kingdom and his righteousness, and all these things will be given to you as well. Therefore do not worry about tomorrow, for tomorrow will worry about itself" (Matthew 6:31, 33–34).

6. COMPETITION

How you can conquer competition:

- Base your personal acceptance on being accepted by Christ.

- Consider individual weaknesses as God's opportunities.

- Relinquish your desire for control to God's sovereignty.

- Derive joy from the Lord and the success of others.

Paul experienced competition from others who preached the gospel:

"Some preach Christ out of envy and rivalry, but others out of goodwill. . . . But what does it matter? The important thing is that in every way, whether from false motives or true, Christ is preached. And because of this I rejoice. Yes, and I will continue to rejoice" (Philippians 1:15, 18).

7. CONSCIENCE

How you can conquer conscience:

- Give God first place in every activity.

- Turn to God as the resource for meeting every need.

- Respond to the needs of others.

- Confess sinful thoughts and acts to God and change sinful ways.

Paul addressed the need of having and maintaining a clear conscience:

"I strive always to keep my conscience clear before God and man" (Acts 24:16).

Write from the Heart

Which of the Bible verses mentioned in this section speak into your life right now? What encouragement do they offer you?

- Conflict (Romans 15:5–7)

- Crisis (Psalm 139:16)

- Change (Daniel 2:20–21)

- Condemnation (Colossians 3:13)

- Concerns (Matthew 6:31, 33–34)

- Competition (Philippians 1:15, 18)

- Conscience (Acts 24:16)

Describe how reducing stress would impact your life (for example, your marriage, parenting, friendships, school and/or work).

....

....

....

....

....

....

....

....

....

....

....

....

Learn from failures—they can be more valuable than successes.

How to Stop Stress with Truth

Lie #1: "The more I do for God, the more He will love me."

TRUTH: God already loves you completely. Nothing you can do will increase His love for you.

"I have loved you with an everlasting love; I have drawn you with unfailing kindness" (Jeremiah 31:3).

Lie #2: "I will lose God's love if I fail."

TRUTH: God's love is always with you regardless of what you do.

"For I am convinced that neither death nor life, neither angels nor demons, neither the present nor the future, nor any powers, neither height nor depth, nor anything else in all creation, will be able to separate us from the love of God that is in Christ Jesus our Lord" (Romans 8:38–39).

God's love is always with you regardless of what you do.

Lie #3: "When I'm not pleasing God, He will condemn me."

TRUTH: God's heart for you is not condemnation. He desires freedom for you and condemns only the sin that has you in bondage.

"There is now no condemnation for those who are in Christ Jesus, because through Christ Jesus the law of the Spirit who gives life has set you free from the law of sin and death" (Romans 8:1–2).

Lie #4: "If I fail, God will punish me."

TRUTH: God does not punish us. He disciplines us for our good that we may share in His holiness.

"They disciplined us for a little while as they thought best; but God disciplines us for our good, in order that we may share his holiness" (Hebrews 12:10).

Lie #5: "Because God is always available when anyone needs Him, I should be too."

TRUTH: Jesus was not always available. He consistently left the crowds and His disciples to be alone and pray.

"After leaving them, he went up on a mountainside to pray" (Mark 6:46).

Lie #6: "To burn out for a cause is admirable."

TRUTH: God never applauds burnout, only balance—a balance of work, rest, play, and prayer.

"There is a time for everything, and a season for every activity under the heavens" (Ecclesiastes 3:1).

Lie #7: "I am not serving God if I'm not seeing tangible results."

TRUTH: You are to serve God in the way He chooses, but you are not responsible for God's timing or the results.

"So neither the one who plants nor the one who waters is anything, but only God, who makes things grow" (1 Corinthians 3:7).

Lie #8: "If I don't do everything that I'm asked to do at church, I'm letting God down."

TRUTH: God is far more interested in having an intimate relationship with you than He is in what you do.

"Jesus replied, 'Love the Lord your God with all your heart and with all your soul and with all your mind.' This is the first and greatest commandment. And a second is like it: 'Love your neighbor as yourself'" (Matthew 22:37–39).

Lie #9: "Life is such a burden, I cannot possibly be happy."

TRUTH: Life is a gift that God wants you to accept with a joyful spirit.

"Moreover, when God gives someone wealth and possessions, and the ability to enjoy them, to accept their lot and be happy in their toil—this is a gift of God" (Ecclesiastes 5:19).

Lie #10: "I must appear to have it together and not allow my mistakes to show."

TRUTH: A spirit of humility is more impressive than a spirit of pride.

"For those who exalt themselves will be humbled, and those who humble themselves will be exalted" (Matthew 23:12).

Lie #11: "Keeping God's laws is the heart of the Christian message."

TRUTH: Reflecting God's grace is the heart of the Christian message.

"I consider my life worth nothing to me; my only aim is to finish the race and complete the task the Lord Jesus has given me—the task of testifying to the good news of God's grace" (Acts 20:24).

Lie #12: "When I'm at death's door, I'll be sorry I didn't accomplish more."

TRUTH: When you're at death's door, your primary regret may be that you didn't show your love more.

"Let no debt remain outstanding, except the continuing debt to love one another, for whoever loves others has fulfilled the law" (Romans 13:8).

Life is a gift that God wants you to accept with a joyful spirit.

Write from the Heart

Read through the list of lies and truths again. Is there a particular lie you are prone to believe? In addition to the Bible verses mentioned in this section, list some other Bible verses or scriptural truths that can combat that lie.

Discussion/Application Questions

1. What are some other lies that people often believe that can cause stress?

   ....

   ....

   ....

   ....

   ....

2. What obstacles (mental, emotional, physical, spiritual, relational, etc.) do people often face when trying to reduce stress in their lives? What obstacles do you face?

   ....

   ....

   ....

   ....

   ....

   ....

3. What habits do you need to begin, change, or quit to help you relieve stress in your life? What would it look like for you to do this?

....

....

....

....

....

....

....

4. What is the first step you can take this week to better manage stress in your life? Is there anyone you need to forgive or is there any unresolved anger in your life? Take some time to share your concerns with the Lord in a written prayer.

....

....

....

....

....

....

....

Notes

"Now may the Lord of peace himself give you
peace at all times and in every way."
2 Thessalonians 3:16

BIBLICAL STEPS TO SOLUTION
PART 2

*"In my distress I called to the LORD; I cried
to my God for help. From his temple
he heard my voice; my cry came
before him, into his ears."*

PSALM 18:6

Reliance Upon God

Lincoln reduced the stress in his life by focusing on what he believed was his divine calling—reuniting a bloodied and devastated country. He also prayed earnestly and constantly. From the executive mansion on May 9, 1864, Lincoln wrote the following letter to Union supporters:

> *"Enough is known of army operations within the last five days to claim our special gratitude to God. While what remains undone demands our most serious prayers to and reliance upon Him (without whom all human effort is vain), I recommend that all patriots, at their homes, at their places of public worship, and wherever they may be, unite in common thanksgiving and prayer to Almighty God."*[21]

Lincoln found relief from his stress through prayer. Talking to God is perhaps the greatest stress-reliever, but God has given us many different avenues to help us reduce stress. In this session, we'll look at stress-reducing techniques and how to relieve excess stress.

The following section is a list of activities that can help do exactly that—cut out stress. Don't think of this as another "to-do" list—that would only create more stress! Rather, think of the list as a set of gifts that God has given us to show us how to handle the stress in our lives.

Stress-Reducing Techniques

1. PRAYER[22]

- Quiet prayer and meditation activates neural structures involved in attention and control of the autonomic nervous system.

- The psalms reflect many heartfelt prayers: Psalm 27:7–14; 31:1–5; 51:1–10; single-verse prayers include: Psalm 51:12; 56:3; 63:1.

  "LORD, hear my prayer, listen to my cry for mercy; in your faithfulness and righteousness come to my relief" (Psalm 143:1).

2. EXERCISE

- Exercise releases the "good" chemicals (such as dopamine and endorphins) and reduces the "bad" (such as cortisol).[23]

- Make a commitment to exercise (walking, swimming, biking) a minimum of 20 minutes a day, three times a week. Mark your progress on a monthly calendar.

  "The wisdom of the prudent is to give thought to their ways, but the folly of fools is deception" (Proverbs 14:8).

3. WRITING

- Take about 20 to 30 minutes a day to write in a private journal. Pour out your honest and open thoughts and feelings to God.

- Give no thought to grammar or spelling. Record your thoughts as they come.

  "Trust in him at all times, you people; pour out your hearts to him, for God is our refuge" (Psalm 62:8).

4. THANKSGIVING

- Make a list of past blessings—answered prayers and acts of kindness by others that lift your spirit, warm your heart, and create within you a sense of goodwill and hopefulness.

- Identify someone each week for whom you are grateful and write a short thank you note or give them a call or text expressing your appreciation for them.

  "For everything God created is good, and nothing is to be rejected if it is received with thanksgiving" (1 Timothy 4:4).

Make a list of blessings!

5. TALKING

- Find someone you trust and consider wise and mature who will agree to be a sounding board for you.

- Meet on a regular basis (either weekly or as often as needed) and share your stressors, listing each one and exploring the reasons they are stressors in your life. Describe your thoughts, feelings, and any traumatic events surrounding them in an open and honest way, not needing to edit your thoughts or weigh your words.

  "I am a woman who is deeply troubled. I have not been drinking wine or beer; I was pouring out my soul to the LORD. Do not take your servant for a wicked woman; I have been praying here out of my great anguish and grief" (1 Samuel 1:15–16).

6. FORGIVENESS

- Make a list of those who have hurt or offended you during your lifetime. Beside their names, write their offenses and the ways you were negatively impacted by them. Record your feelings surrounding each event and the pain and stress you have carried as a result.

- Share your list with the Lord and then go back over it again, this time releasing each person, the offense, and all your pain to Him. Trust Him to deal with the people, their offenses, and your pain as He sees fit. Lastly, dispose of the list, showing that you have released it all into the Lord's hands.

  "Bear with each other and forgive one another if any of you has a grievance against someone. Forgive as the Lord forgave you" (Colossians 3:13).

Write from the Heart

Read 2 Corinthians 1:3–11. Times of suffering are always stressful. Based on this passage, what did the apostle Paul do to reduce the level of stress he was experiencing?

....

....

....

....

....

....

Describe how one or two of the stress-reducing techniques mentioned so far (#1–6) would be or have been helpful to you or someone you know.

....

....

....

....

....

....

....

7. TOUCH

- Find a good massage therapist and get a massage on a regular basis when stress is bearing down on you.

- Make a conscious effort to touch the people in your life either by giving them a pat on the back, a hug, or a gentle squeeze on the arm or hand. Play games with family and friends that involve playful and gentle touch. "Roughhouse" with your children—rolling on the ground together, crawling over each other, or hoisting them onto your shoulders.

  "Greet one another with a holy kiss" (2 Corinthians 13:12).

8. HUMOR

- Plan fun-filled times on a regular basis with family, friends, and coworkers in an effort to relieve stress or avoid stress buildup.

- Play fun games with loved ones, watch funny movies or sitcoms, read a funny story, share humorous events from your life at least once a month or whenever stress is knocking at your door or the door of someone you care about.

  "He will yet fill your mouth with laughter and your lips with shouts of joy" (Job 8:21).

9. SCRIPTURE

- "May these words of my mouth and this meditation of my heart be pleasing in your sight, LORD, my Rock and my Redeemer" (Psalm 19:14).

- "The LORD is my light and my salvation—whom shall I fear? The LORD is the stronghold of my life—of whom shall I be afraid?" (Psalm 27:1).

- "The LORD is close to the brokenhearted and saves those who are crushed in spirit" (Psalm 34:18).

- "Why, my soul, are you downcast? Why so disturbed within me? Put your hope in God, for I will yet praise him, my Savior and my God" (Psalm 42:5).

- "My sacrifice, O God, is a broken spirit; a broken and contrite heart you, God, will not despise" (Psalm 51:17).

- "The LORD is my strength and my shield; my heart trusts in him, and he helps me. My heart leaps for joy, and with my song I praise him" (Psalm 28:7).

- "Do not fret because of those who are evil or be envious of those who do wrong" (Psalm 37:1).

- "I waited patiently for the LORD; he turned to me and heard my cry" (Psalm 40:1).

- "Hear me, LORD, and answer me, for I am poor and needy" (Psalm 86:1).

10. MEDITATION

- Simple meditation can involve sitting up straight with your eyes closed for 10 or 20 minutes. Establish a breathing rhythm by breathing in slowly through your nose and exhaling completely through your mouth. As you continue to do this, repeat one word or a short phrase of Scripture, over and over.

    "I trust in you . . . " (Psalm 25:2).

    "The LORD is my strength . . . " (Psalm 28:7).

    "You are my hiding place . . . " (Psalm 32:7).

- Repeat this exercise again sometime during the day.

11. MUSIC

- Listen to classical or praise music.

- Sing inspirational praise music.

    "Sing to the LORD with grateful praise; make music to our God on the harp" (Psalm 147:7).

12. EATING

- Eat at least three meals a day or five small ones. Don't skip or forget meals.

- Avoid fast food, sweets, alcohol, and caffeine. Too much caffeine can have a negative impact on your body when you're under stress. Caffeine impacts the hormones in your body, causing an increase in hormones, such as adrenaline, cortisol, and dopamine.

"Then God said, 'I give you every seed-bearing plant on the face of the whole earth and every tree that has fruit with seed in it. They will be yours for food'" (Genesis 1:29).

Write from the Heart

Look at the Bible verses mentioned in this section. Copy the ones that speak to your current situation the most. Then describe how one or two of the stress-reducing techniques (#7–12) would be or have been helpful to you.

How to Relieve Stress Overload

STOP

Stop and look at the real reason you are experiencing stress.

- Do I try to meet my own needs instead of waiting on the Lord?

- Do I think God cannot get along without me?

- Do I seek self-worth through proving my adequacy and effectiveness?

- Am I Spirit-led or people-pressured?

  "Am I now trying to win the approval of human beings, or of God? Or am I trying to please people? If I were still trying to please people, I would not be a servant of Christ" (Galatians 1:10).

Stop, confess, and turn away from any known sin in your life.

- Do I manipulate or control others?

- Do I feel envious or jealous of others?

- Do I express my feelings inappropriately?

- Do I overreact to criticism?

- Do I have impure motives?

  "Whoever conceals their sins does not prosper, but the one who confesses and renounces them finds mercy" (Proverbs 28:13).

YIELD

Yield to God's sovereign control over your circumstances.

- What is God doing in my circumstances?

- In what way does God want me to change?

- How does God want me to respond?

- Do I have impure motives?

  "In the LORD's hand the king's heart is a stream of water that he channels toward all who please him" (Proverbs 21:1).

Yield to God your perceived rights and your expectations.

- I yield my right to control my circumstances.

- I yield my right to be accepted by others.

- I yield my right to be successful.

- I yield my right to be heard and understood.

- I yield my right to be right.

  "Trust in the LORD with all your heart and lean not on your own understanding" (Proverbs 3:5).

RESUME SPEED

Resume speed, living in the presence of God.

"Dear Lord,

- I choose to let Christ live His life through me.

- I choose to live in the present, not worrying about tomorrow. I choose to refocus my thoughts from my pressures to Your purposes for allowing this pressure.

- I choose to make a commitment to talk less and listen more.

- I choose to have a thankful heart regardless of the pressure I feel.

- I will call on You, Lord, for wisdom and peace."

  "Blessed are those who have learned to acclaim you, who walk in the light of your presence, LORD" (Psalm 89:15).

Live in the presence of God.

A Model to Follow

Toward the end of his life, Lincoln modeled how to relieve unhealthy stress and how to bless others in the midst of stressful circumstances.

Relieving stress begins with a right relationship with God through His Son, Jesus Christ, and understanding that God is sovereign over everything. There is no better stress reliever than knowing that God is in control of *every* circumstance in our lives.

Next, reading and studying God's Word and spending time with God in prayer was a great relief to Lincoln. He was undoubtedly comforted by the assurances from God's Word about His infinite love, grace, and eagerness to help and save.

Lastly, Lincoln was greatly relieved when he understood that his life had purpose. Realizing your life has purpose can be a great stress reducer. Lincoln furthermore understood that he could never fulfill his purpose in his own strength, but through God's strength alone.

Discussion/Application Questions

1. Over the past six sessions, how has your understanding of stress changed as a result of this study? What are one or two key takeaways the Lord has revealed to you about handling stress?

....

....

....

....

....

....

2. Describe the benefits (physical, mental, emotional, spiritual, relational) of implementing some of the stress-reducing techniques listed in this session.

....

....

....

....

....

....

3. Take a moment and list some of the good things God has done in your life during stressful times. Thank Him for the moments that have helped you grow and taught you more about Him.

....

....

....

....

....

....

....

4. As you look ahead, describe at least one key step you will take or one habit in your life that will begin, change, or stop in order to help you reduce stress in your life.

....

....

....

....

....

....

....

....

5. Psalm 68:19 says, "Praise be to the Lord, to God our Savior, who daily bears our burdens." Take some time to praise God for daily bearing your burdens and walking with you through this study. Write down all the reasons for which you can praise and thank God.

....

....

....

....

....

....

....

....

....

....

....

There is no better stress reliever than knowing that God is in control.

Notes

Notes

"Now may the Lord of peace himself give you
peace at all times and in every way."
2 Thessalonians 3:16

Endnotes

1. Joshua Wolf Shenk, *Lincoln's Melancholy* (New York: Houghton Mifflin, 2005), 18.

2. Shenk, *Lincoln's Melancholy*, 21.

3. John D. Woodbridge, *More Than Conquerors* (Chicago: Moody, 1992) "Savior of a Nation," 16.

4. Merriam Webster Online Dictionary, s.v. "Distress."

5. W. E. Vine, Merrill F. Unger, and William White, Jr., *Vine's Complete Expository Dictionary of Biblical Words*, electronic ed. (Nashville: Thomas Nelson, 1996), s.v. "Distress."

6. Shenk, *Lincoln's Melancholy*, 43.

7. Shenk, *Lincoln's Melancholy*, 44.

8. Shenk, *Lincoln's Melancholy*, 51.

9. Shenk, *Lincoln's Melancholy*, 95.

10. Shenk, *Lincoln's Melancholy*, 96.

11. Shenk, *Lincoln's Melancholy*, 56.

12. Lloyd John Ogilvie, *Making Stress Work for You: Ten Proven Principles* (Waco, TX: Word, 1985). (Ogilvie divides stress causes under the headings: change, conflict, criticism, concerns, and crises.)

13. Don Warrick, *How to Handle Stress*, (Colorado Springs, CO: NavPress, 1989), 5–6.

14. Warrick, *How to Handle Stress*, 6.

15. Warrick, *How to Handle Stress*, 6–7.

16. Shenk, *Lincoln's Melancholy*, 55.

17. Shenk, *Lincoln's Melancholy*, 65.

18. Carl Sandburg, *Lincoln's Melancholy*, (New York: Sterling, 2007), 122.

19. Shenk, *Lincoln's Melancholy*, 186.

20. Shenk, *Lincoln's Melancholy*, 193.

21. Abraham Lincoln, *Abraham Lincoln's Pen and Voice* (Cincinnati: R. Clarke and Co., 1890), 360.

22. Herbert Benson and William Proctor, *The Break-Out Principle* (New York: Scribner, 2003), 69–73.

23. Julia Ross, *The Mood Cure* (New York: Penguin, 2004), 32.

HOPE FOR THE HEART
Biblically Based Studies on Everyday Issues
6-Session Bible Studies

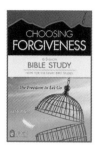

CHOOSING FORGIVENESS
Learn how you can be an expression of God's grace by forgiving others and find the freedom He intended you to have.
ISBN: 9781628623840

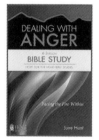

DEALING WITH ANGER
Have you ever reacted rashly out of anger—and lived to regret it? You can learn to keep your anger under control and learn how to act rather than react.
ISBN: 9781628623871

OVERCOMING DEPRESSION
Can anything dispel the darkness of depression? The answer is yes! Let God lead you through the storm and into the light.
ISBN: 9781628623901

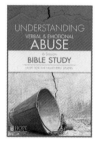

UNDERSTANDING VERBAL AND EMOTIONAL ABUSE
You can learn biblical truths and practical "how to's" for stopping the pain of abuse and for restoring peace in all your relationships.
ISBN: 9781628623932

HANDLING STRESS
Discover biblical approaches to handling stress. God wants to be your source of calm in stressful situations.
ISBN: 9781628623963

FINDING SELF-WORTH IN CHRIST
Learn to leave behind feelings of worthlessness, and experience the worth you have in the eyes of your heavenly Father.
ISBN: 9781628623994

www.HendricksonRose.com • www.AspirePress.com